The Secret

The first thing to be thrust into your face as a newborn baby is likely to be a Teddy Bear. Despite the usual juvenile introduction (a wiggling of the Bear from side-to-side accompanied by the words "coochy coochy coo"), Teddy will probably remain a pal and confidante throughout the child's early years. Yet how many parents stop to think of the long-term consequences of this seemingly harmless alliance?

A general assumption among 'grown-ups' is one of a Teddy providing comfort to a young child. Whilst this belief is partly correct, there are also some less desirable spin-offs, from THE SECRET LIVES OF TEDDY BEARS. Some observers would say the unruly behaviour of adolescents today can be directly attributed to wayward Teddies leading young children astray.

Take a look through this exposé and decide for yourself; wouldn't your child be better off with a rubber duck?

TEDDY BEARS

The Secret Lives of

Other humour titles from R&B Publishing:

How to Train Your Cat

The Hangover Handbook and Beerlover's Bible

The Ancient Art of Farting

Written by Edward Nude
Illustrated by C.Uddly

RB

R&B Publishing
P.O.Box 200
Harrogate
HG2 9RB

TEDDY BEARS

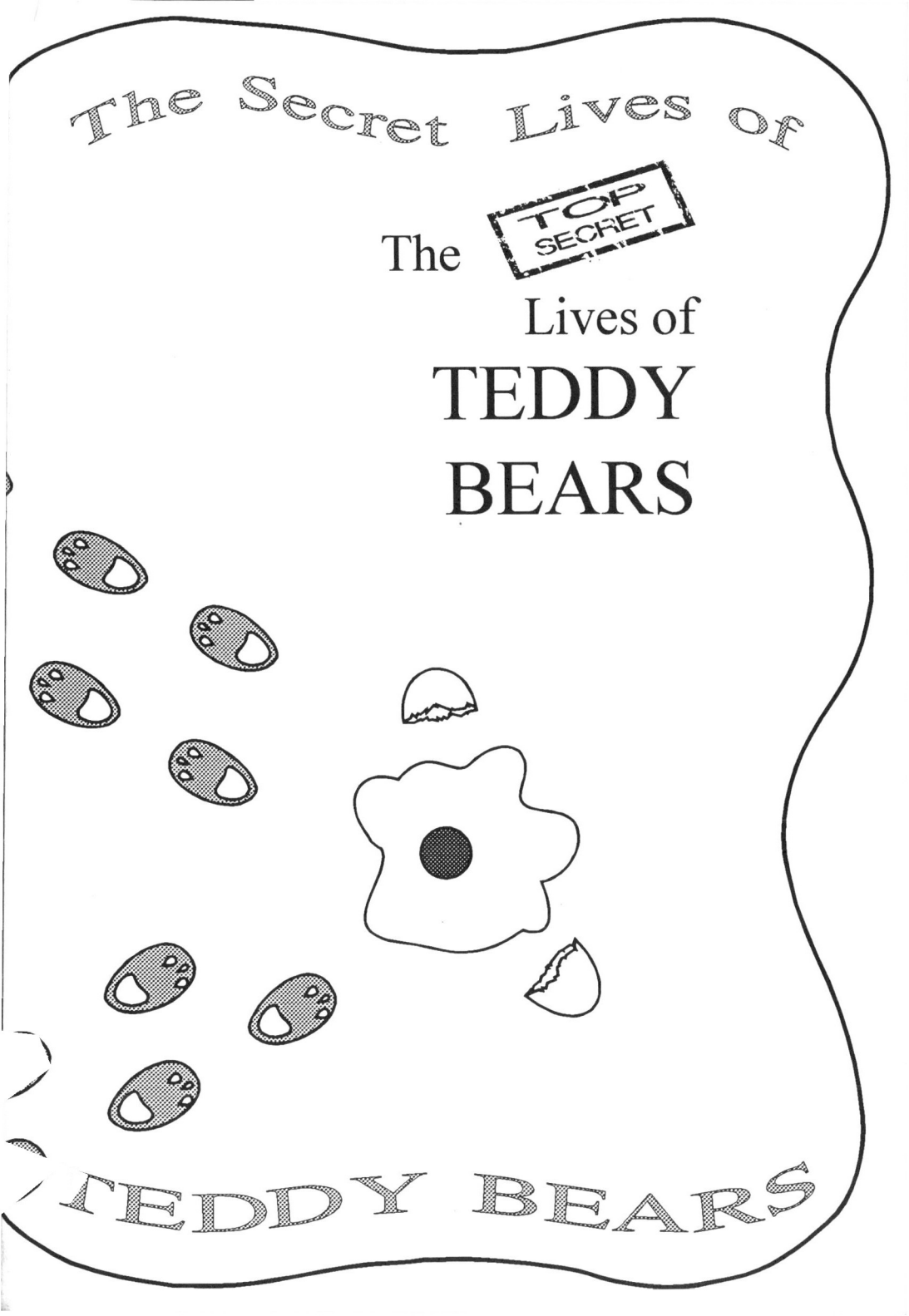

The Secret Lives of

The ~~TOP SECRET~~ Lives of

TEDDY BEARS

TEDDY BEARS

The Secret Lives of

R&B is an imprint of:-
R&B Publishing
P.O.Box 200
Harrogate
HG2 9RB
England
Tel/Fax:(0423)507545

Copyright ©1992 R&B Publishing

First Published in October 1992 by R&B Publishing,

Australasian Edition:
MaxiBooks
P.O.Box 268
Springwood
NSW 2777
Australia
Tel:(047)514967, Fax:(047)515545

All rights reserved. No part of this publication may be reproduced, stored in a retrieval system, or transmitted in any form or by any means, electronic, mechanical, photocopying, recording or otherwise (by Humans or Teddy Bears), without the prior written permission of the publishers.

ISBN 1-873668-01-5

Illustrations, typesetting and design by:
Impact Designs, P.O.Box 200, Harrogate, HG2 9RB.

Printed and bound in Spain by Grafos S.A., Barcelona.

British Library Cataloguing-in-Publication Data:
A catalogue record for this book is
available from the British Library

Teddy Bears

The Secret Lives of

IN THE BEGINNING

The first biblical Teddy Bears belonged to Adam and Eve. Unable to open his eyes, Adam's favourite pastime was curling up with his thumb in his mouth while cuddling his furry pal. That was until his Bear took exception to the juvenile behaviour of sucking thumbs. One night the Bear slipped out of bed, grabbed an apple off the closest tree of knowledge, removed Adam's thumb and stuffed the apple in its place.

God wasn't very happy with the Bear's prankish behaviour and condemned all Teddy Bears to appear inanimate in the presence of Humans. In fact he decreed that they should freeze as soon as any human lay eyes on them. From thence on, Teddy Bears have had to lead secret lives.

It is this restriction on our furry friends' movements which has perverted their sense of humour even further. In an effort to keep their brains occupied* they have developed their pranks into something approaching an art form.

* Although a Teddy's brain is lighter than a humans', he generally uses more of it.

TEDDY BEARS

The Secret Lives of

PREHISTORIC PRANKS

The earliest trick performed by a Teddy was carried out by an enormous Bear called Brontedbearaurus. This Teddy is widely held to be the first species of cuddly toy that can readily be identified as belonging to the family *Tyeddus Furbearex*, to which all modern Teddy Bears belong. The Brontobear, as it is more commonly known, roamed the earth approximately 70 million years ago.

Measuring more than 28 metres in length, this giant Bear weighed approximately 25 tonnes and lived in a gigantic prehistoric bed made from Pterodactyl feathers. The Brontobear was a sleeping companion for most of the dinosaurs, except for the intelligent Adultasaurus who could see the bad influence it was having on reptile-kind.

This influence came to a head when all the Brontobears conspired to pull pranks simultaneously on their dinosaur owners. One night they planted the subliminal idea of a day trip to seaside. Once there, the Brontobears ran off with all the dinosaur's clothes and placed them further up the beach. Unable to see their clothes, the gigantic reptiles were forced to stay in the sea to preserve their modesty, where they all subsequently drowned and became extinct.

TEDDY BEARS

The Secret Lives of TEDDY BEARS

"TYEDDUS" FURBEAREX

The Secret Lives of

FROZEN BEAR

The first example of a more recognisable and more normally sized Teddy Bear was found preserved in a glacier in the mountains of Austria. This Bear, around 4,000 years old, was perfectly preserved and still dressed in little clothes which its owner's mother had made for it.

It was holding a set of car keys, which it was obviously in the course of hiding from the owner. In itself, this fact isn't too surprising to historians who have known of the mischievous nature of Teddy Bears for a long time. More puzzling is the complete lack of a sofa cushion for hiding the keys behind.

TEDDY TRUTH
The short form of Teddy is 'Ted', which means to turn over and dry; like hay.

The age of this Austrian Bear was set by radioactive carbon dating techniques. However, it is a particularly inaccurate procedure for putting an age on a Teddy Bear for two reasons. Firstly, Teddies regularly gain access to scientific laboratories and change the data. Secondly, Teddies aren't made from carbon because it would make your bedsheets go black.

TEDDY BEARS

The Secret Lives of TEDDY BEARS

The Secret Lives of

SEX, TEDS AND ROCK 'N ROLL

Most Teddies, of course, come as males and females. However, the naughty Bears which are re-fured to in these pages are almost always the males of the species - those Bears with an extra dangly piece of cotton. So throughout the rest of the book, Teddy is refurred to in the masculine gender. The publishers apologise for any distress this may cause members of the feminist organisation Spare Stitch.

It may come as a bit of an 'eye opener' to learn that Teddy Bears procreate (where do you think all those little Teddies come from ?). But rest assured, your eyes would open a lot wider if you actually caught your Teddy Bear at it. You wouldn't get much thanks from your Bears either. Having to freeze all movement in the middle of a bit of nookie is a touch disconcerting, and is termed *"Bearus Interuptus"*.

Some Teddies are hermaphroditic, but most depend on the results of a simple orgy for their reproduction. Put two Bears of the opposite sex together and turn your back for more than a minute, then listen carefully for little squeals of furry goings-on. If anybody complains about your bed-sheets being ruffled, blame it on your Teddy Bears having it away.

Last, but certainly not least, always check your condom if there is a Teddy around. Bears simply love putting their claws through the silver foil and making minute holes in the rubber.

TEDDY BEARS

The Secret Lives of

SQUELCH!

TEDDY BEARS

The Secret Lives of

CHEAP LABOUR

The Teddy population of the world has been steadily increasing since Teddies were first made. But more recently growth has been tending towards exponential, with a boom in oriental Bears flooding the market.

These Teddies, usually shorter than the normal Teddy, originate in the Far East and find their way into this country hidden in crates to avoid the attentions of customs officers. They can be readily identified by their short stubby legs, and a thin line of stitching for their eyes rather than the usual glass bead.

Once in the country these unfortunate Bears are put to work for a pittance by their new heartless owners. Have you ever wondered how all those letters that are posted get franked? Small slave Bears from the orient are employed to run along rows of letters with ink on their paws, franking the letters as they go. The only rest these Bears get in an average 24 hour shift, is when the Post Office owners let them sit down while the date is changed on the bottom of their paws. Nearer Christmas, with the high volumes of mail sent, spare a thought for the P.O. Bears who are often made to work more than 36 hours a day !

TEDDY TRUTH
Arctophiles are people who collect Teddy Bears. The name is derived from "Arctos", the Greek for bear.

TEDDY BEARS

The Secret Lives of

TEDDY BEARS

The Secret Lives of

(Bear wearing a shirt labeled "FRIDGE LIGHT ATTENDANT")

TEDDY BEARS

The Secret Lives of TEDDY BEARS

The Secret Lives of

FIRST PAWS

A TRUE TEDDY STORY

DID YOU KNOW the Teddy Bear was named after Theodore Roosevelt (1858-1919) who was the 26th president of the United States (1901-9). The original Teddy was better known for his vigorous regulation of big business by 'trust busting', and for gaining the Nobel Peace Prize for mediation in the Russo-Japanese War.

On a trip to sort out a boundary dispute between the states of Louisiana and Mississippi, Theodore was taken on a Bear hunting trip. Despite being an accomplished hunter, the president failed to shoot a single Bear. Wanting to keep the president happy, his helpers caught a young Bear, tied it with a rope by the neck and secured it near the president's tent. Minutes later they ran into the tent shouting "Bear, Bear".

The president rushed out with his gun to see the young defenceless Bear cub tied close by. Apparently having no taste for an easy kill and a shrewd eye on the media circus following him, he turned round and said "If I shoot this Bear, I could never look my children in the eye again".

Next day, most of the papers carried the story. One of them, the Washington Star, also printed a cartoon by Clyfford

TEDDY BEARS

The Secret Lives of

Berryman showing the president refusing to kill the young Bear who had taken on some human characteristics.

A shopkeeping Russian immigrant in Brooklyn called Morris Mitchom saw the cartoon. He thought it would be a good idea to make a stuffed toy imitation of the Bear shown in the cartoon, and got his wife to make one. Within hours of the Bear going in his shop window to attract customers, someone offered to buy it. Before long Mrs Mitchom was working day and night to supply the orders for her toy Bears.

TEDDY BEARS

The Secret Lives of

SWORN ENEMIES

Teddy's biggest enemy in most households is the pet cat. Not only does the dreaded moggy vie for the owner's attention and affection, it also has a habit of pouncing on Ted while he is up to his pranks.

With the desire to jump on anything that moves deeply entrenched in the cat's genes, Teddy is a natural target. This prompts even more caution from Ted. One bite from the cat may not cause too much damage to a Bear, but a slash from the claws can mean a severe loss of stuffing and an emergency operation with the sewing machine.

Not surprisingly, a lot of Teddy's pranks are designed to get the feline fiend into trouble as a scapegoat. The disappearance of food from a table can invariably bring a sore head to the cat and a smirk on Teddy's face.

Several more enterprising Teddies have set up a cottage industry to help Bears throughout the country. They manufacture rubber stamps in the shape of a cat's paw. Any Teddy can purchase one of these pads for a small amount of cash. All they have to do is put the stamp in some mud, leave a trail all the way to some Teddy-created damage, and hey presto ! - a kick for the cat.

TEDDY BEARS

The Secret Lives of TEDDY BEARS

The Secret Lives of

BEARS AND SPIRITS

Is your house inhabited by ghosts, or have you seen any apparitions wandering around with their heads stuck under their arms? If you believe poltergeists and the like are living it up in your abode, it is probably at the invitation of your Teddy Bears.

Ghosts are, in fact, very timid and don't like to come over from the 'other side'. But liking a good old joke themselves, they are often tempted by a particularly mischievous Teddy. Of course, once the ghost has been tempted into a prank it is likely to find the Teddy has done a disappearing act to leave the ghost to take all the blame. Teddy would say something like

TEDDY TRUTH
The most well known Teddies are made by Steiff and Bing in Germany, and Chad Valley and Merrythought in Britain

"Wouldn't it be a good idea if we knocked this picture off the wall", knowing full well he couldn't reach it on his own. The ghost would breeze over to the picture, totally oblivious to Teddy slipping back into bed. Just as the ghost knocks the picture down, Ted gives his owner a good boot in the ribs so he or she wakes up and says "What was that" or better still screams the house down.

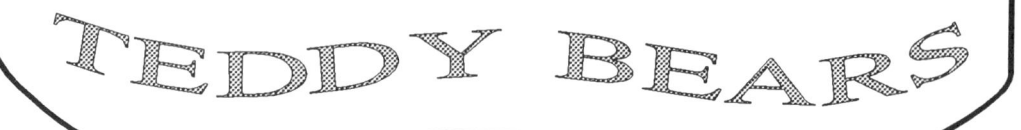

TEDDY BEARS

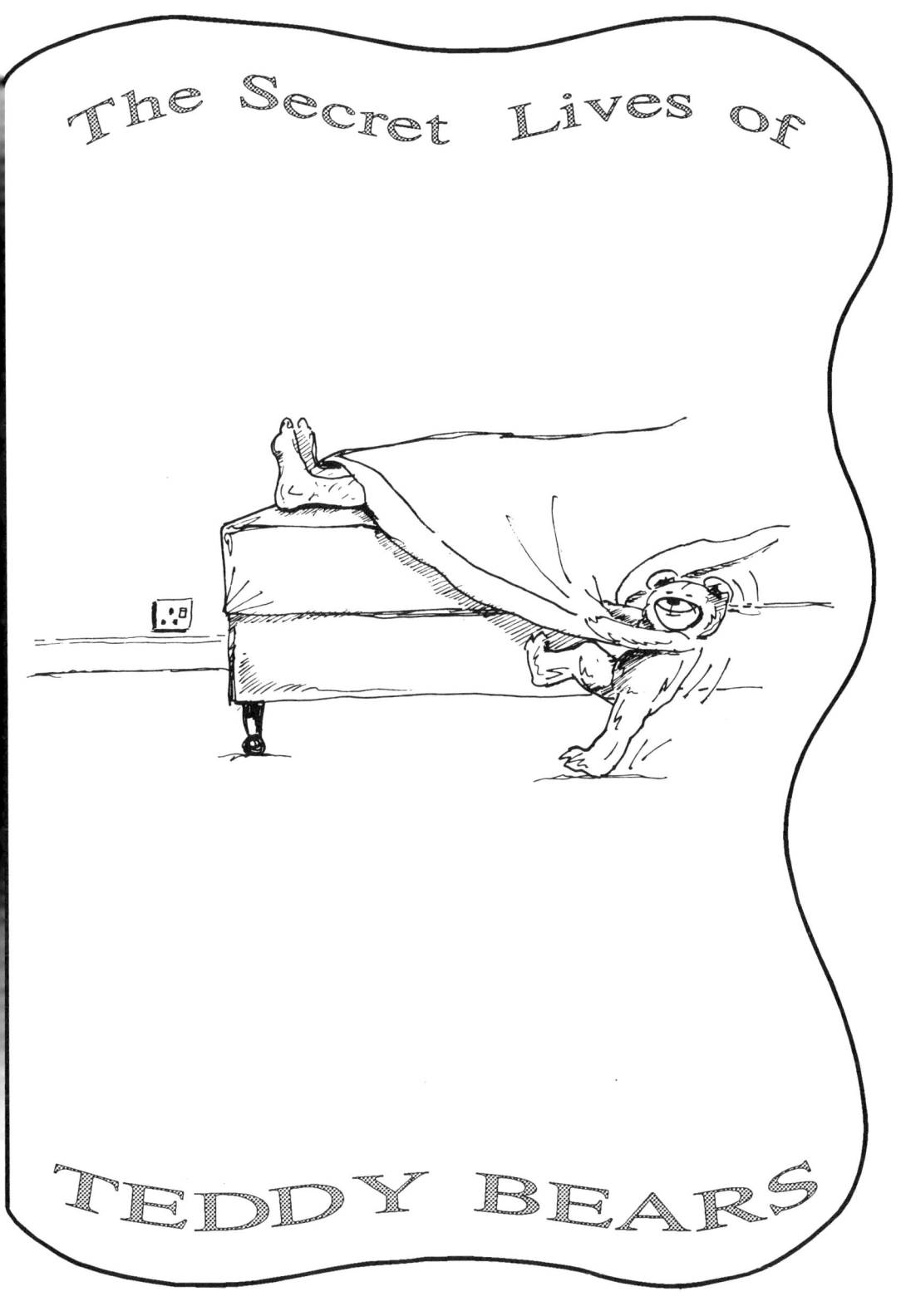

The Secret Lives of

TEDDY BEARS

The Secret Lives of

RISING CRIME IN SNUGGLEONIA

Has your Teddy ever invited you to the secret land of Snuggleonia? If not, don't be too concerned. Not only do you need to be a very close trusted friend of your Teddy, but you need to have performed some great feat for Teddy-kind. Anyway, you probably wouldn't want to go there at present.

Snuggleonia is a parallel universe inhabited solely by Teddy Bears. Until recently it has been a very soft and pleasant place to live. The Bear's houses are made from pillows and all the roads are covered in cotton sheets.

But all is not well in this apparent heaven. The ready availability of EcstaTeddy, a banned narcotic which makes you feel as hard as a Human, has caused an outbreak of pawlessness.

Gangs of Furheads, who have shaved their fur down to the Bear seams, are roaming around terrorising Snugglonia's inhabitants. Even the upholders of the paw, the Pawlice, have stopped padding the beat and only go out in their pandas.

TEDDY TRUTH

Do not confuse Teddy Bears with Teddy Boys who prefer to dress in a style characteristic of the reign of Edward VIII of England (1901-10). Teddy Girls are widely accepted to copy Teddy Boys in behaviour but not in dress.

TEDDY BEARS

The Secret Lives of
TEDDY BEARS

The Secret Lives of

IN THE WOODS TONIGHT

If you go down to the woods tonight you certainly will be in for a big surprise. For every Bear, that ever there was, will be gathered for a House Party. No longer will a simple picnic suffice, the modern day Teddy wants to get a rush the same as everyone else. You also wouldn't find them gathered in a quiet opening amongst the trees, they are more likely to be found in a new warehouse that has been built on the green-belt.

Although Inter-Bear has put extra officers onto the case in an effort to stop these parties taking place for 'safety reasons' (they weren't invited), the Bears are winning the battle by only organising their parties at the last minute. There is no point asking your Teddy where he is going to party on-down, because he won't tell you. An hour before the party starts, your Bear will receive a 'phone call to tell him where the party's at (have you ever woken up thinking you've heard the 'phone ring ?).

Minutes later your Teddy will put his glad-rags on, rub in a dob of sinus clearer and take a sniff of EcstaTeddy, before heading off into the night. You may also find some cash missing from your savings, since the organisers of the party often charge for each furry entry.

TEDDY BEARS

The Secret Lives of TEDDY BEARS

The Secret Lives of

GORY GOLDILOCKS

A TRUE TEDDY STORY

Everyone knows the children's story of Goldilocks and the Three Bears, about a small girl who wanders into the Bears' house, eats their porridge and sleeps in their beds. But did you know the 'girl' was an 'old woman' in the original story? The ending was rather different as well. Chased and caught by the Bears, the old woman was thrown in a fire and when she survived the Bears tried to drown her. Escaping these first two fates, the old woman was then thrown from a church steeple and eaten by the Bears! **Real Teddy Bears would never behave like this, they prefer chocolate biscuits.**

SAYINGS

Teddies don't talk in the same way as humans, but here are a few things that humans say about them:-

Too many Teddies crowd the bed.
A Teddy Bear in the hand, is worth two in the shop.
A stitch in Teddy, holds him together.
Confucius, he say... where's my Teddy?
One Teddy, doesn't make a collection.
If you break a Teddy, it will bring bad luck for seven years.
Walking under a Teddy is asking for trouble.
If you pull faces when the wind changes direction,
you will end up looking like a Teddy.

TEDDY BEARS

The Secret Lives of

TEDDY BEARS

The Secret Lives of

WHAT'S GOING ON IN TEDDY'S HEAD

If you don't believe your Teddy Bear is up to something, take a good look at his facial expression. Anyone with a grin like that has got to be up to no good. Below is a quick identifier for you to try and work out what prank your Bear may be planning next.

Sticking down envelopes before you put anything in them.

Switching the lights on when you've gone to bed.

Moving the furniture so you trip over it on the way to the toilet at night in the dark.

TEDDY BEARS

The Secret Lives of

*P*ouring water over your biscuits in the air-tight container to make them soggy.

*H*iding the electricity bill so you get cut off.

*S*neaking out to the car and switching on the lights to flatten the battery. Note: the turn up at the corner of the mouth indicates this Bear will go back down just before dawn and put the switch back into the 'off' position.

*P*ulling the cat's tail.

TEDDY BEARS

The Secret Lives of

TEDDY MISDEMEANOURS

Prank	Pleasure Rating
Sleeping with owner	0
Providing comfort in hard times	-1
Being waggled in babies' faces	2
Lying underneath owners to make them uncomfortable	4
Setting alarm off on 'long lie-in' day	8
Looking cute on well made bed	-2
Ruffling of sheets on newly made bed	4
Putting dirty cat-looking paw marks on clean sheets	8
Lifting cat from cat-box and putting it on bed	9
Pinching food and smearing on cat's lips	10
Kicking baby until it wakes	4
Hiding train pass	4
Hiding wallet/purse	6
Smearing lipstick on shirt collars	5
Spraying perfume on same shirt	7
Sending mysterious Valentine cards	2
Creaking doors at night	3
Causing taps to drip	3
Putting plug into sink with tap dripping (depending on when it's discovered)	3 to 9
Putting super-glue on jar lids	6
Draining petrol from car	4
As above plus gluing petrol gauge	8
Intercepting cheques in the post	5
Hiding important telephone numbers	8

TEDDY BEARS

The Secret Lives of TEDDY BEARS

The Secret Lives of

TEDDY'S TIMETABLE

Teddies don't like a set routine - have you ever seen a Teddy with a diary? They prefer to live by reactive scheduling. That is to say, their behaviour depends on what is happening around them.

One 'Old Wives' tale says that problems always come in threes. This is no coincidence, since they are all brought about by the mischievous Teddy Bear. Alerted by you shouting or groaning at a minor or major mishap, the Bear's warped mind will instantaneously think of something with which to follow it up. (Teddy psychologists believe this conduct to be a result of not wanting to be outdone). Invariably Teddy's first prank does not produce the desired result. But his second, following a build-up of tension in his owners' mind, will usually produce plenty of cursing, shouting and throwing of objects. The most favourable of all results, as far as Teddy is concerned, will be a good booting for the cat.

However, there are certain times of the day, and year, when you can expect Teddy's pranks to increase:-

7-9 a.m. A good time for pranks. Owner probably in a rush to get off to work. Hiding of objects always goes down well at this time. Must be careful not to be seen because of lots of aimless running around by owner.

TEDDY BEARS

The Secret Lives of

9 a.m.-Midday Time for sleeping after an active night. Perhaps prepare a few 'bad news' letters or bill for owner's lunchtime.

Midday-2 p.m. Again increased activity if owner comes home. Altering of clocks to make lunch break seem short, reading of 'bad news' letters and tipping of food onto trousers/skirts.

2-5 p.m. Slow time of day. Chase cat around and/or cause a bit of damage and make it look as if the cat has done it. Make list of pranks to do after midnight.

5-7 p.m. Smile at cat. Do whatever is necessary to cause an argument between owners over dinner. Take care not to be seen moving.

7-10 p.m. Prepare for bed while owners watching TV. Squeeze toothpaste tube, hide night clothes, switch off electric blanket and make sure bed is squeaking.

10 p.m.-Midnight Lie in bed and stay still. Too much danger of being spotted.

Midnight-7 a.m. Prepare for next day. Alter clock or alarm; hide all work clothes, clean socks and underwear; disable car; open fridge door; switch lights on; make 'strange' noises; pull cat's tail; alter video recorder settings; have a Bear's party.

TEDDY BEARS

The Secret Lives of Teddy Bears

The pranks Teddy Bears like to play may vary during the year:-

SEASON   **FAVOURITE ACTIVITIES**

Winter A great time for causing leaks by fracturing pipes in the roof. Better if your owner lives in a flat and you can cause a flood in the flat below.

Turn radiators off and alter timer on central heating controls.

Get away with sabotaging the car virtually every night.

Spray inside of windows with water so it freezes. Open other windows to let cold in over night.

Festive Hide Christmas card and presents list. Unscrew fairy lights on Christmas tree, knock over Christmas cards received and stick price labels on presents. Eat chocolates and pull down decorations.

AUGUST						
1X	2X	3X	4	5	6	7
8	9	10	11	12	13	14
15	16		19	20	21	
22	23	24	25	26	27	28

PARTY

The Secret Lives of

Spring

Annoy cat as much as possible during mating season. Break buds off prize roses and any new plants. During 'spring cleaning', pull down newly hung wallpaper, place embarrassing objects to be found by owner's partner and tip bags of dust all over cleaned areas.

Summer

Turn on central heating and blow fuses on air-conditioning units.

Leave fridge and freezer doors open as often as possible. Divert resulting pools of water onto best carpet in the house.

Go absolutely mad during owner's summer holidays. Burgle house; send various 'bad news' telegrams to resort; arrange for an extra specially good financial month at owner's work while they are away; hold a mega-party.

If taken on holiday abroad, put an extra bottle of whisky and some dodgy looking powder into suitcases for return journey. Open camera to over-expose pictures.

Autumn

Mundane chores such as inviting all owner's friends to dinner and erasing all reminders from calenders and diaries, altering crosses on pools entries and annoying the cat. Scattering leaves on newly swept paths.

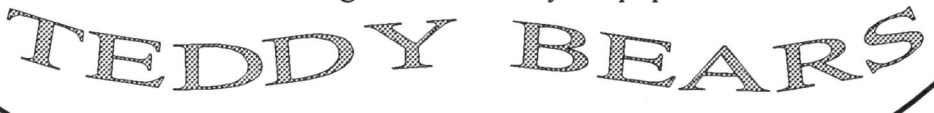

TEDDY BEARS

The Secret Lives of

TEDDY IN THE TUB

When washing your Teddy take great care not to cause him any damage. If you hurt your furry friend, you are likely to regret it for a long time. Teddies never forget and 'retribution' might as well be their middle name.

Putting Teddy in the washing machine for instance, could prove expensive for the rest of your clothes. First of all, you are likely to have trouble actually getting him in. He is liable to spread out his paws so you can't get him through the door. If you do get him in, any other items in there will be ripped to shreds in a fit of temper. The blame, of course, won't fall on Teddy directly but on the sharp parts put in him by cheapskate foreign manufacturers.

All future washes will be doomed to come out with a feint pink hue from the dye he will put in with every load. And that's the items you get back. Most small items, such as single socks, will simply disappear. Since Ted usually lives in the bedroom, he will know which are your favourite clothes, so expect those items to go missing or get damaged first.

TEDDY BEARS

The Secret Lives of
TEDDY BEARS

The Secret Lives of

BEARS AND THE BOX

Not being allowed to be seen moving by humans severely restricts the recreational behaviour of Teddy Bears. Their main activity, when not thinking up pranks, is to watch TV and videos.

Once you are soundly asleep, Teddy will sneak downstairs, call up a few of his friends to come and watch a couple of videos (that's why you will find numbers you don't recognise on your itemised telephone bill). The other Bears will usually bring their own beer, but the host Bear has to provide the chocolate biscuits.

After a few cans as a warm-up, the Bears will reach for the naughty pornography videos. The strange squeaks that you hear during the night can often be attributed to the giggles of the Bears when the alcohol gets into their stuffing.

Most signs of a Teddy video party will be cleared away in the morning. However, you may notice crumbs on the carpet, a smell of stale beer and the video tape you left in the machine will not be rewound. If the Bears got a little drunk and yearned for a prank or two, you may find your favourite video erased and the time altered on the clock.

Note: Some Bears with qualifications in electronics also know how to alter a video recorder so it always records the wrong station or cuts the end off a programme you wanted to see.

TEDDY BEARS

The Secret Lives of TEDDY BEARS

The Secret Lives of

TIME TO SLEEP

One of the most practised pranks pulled by Teddies all over the world is the alteration of clocks. This serves more than one purpose. Primarily it can cause The Owner to be late for work or an important appointment. But it usually also causes The Owner to sleep longer, thereby giving Ted more time to arrange tricks and misdemeanours around the house.

You will have noticed how everything seems to go wrong when you are late. Blame Ted. The extra time gained while you were busy becoming late will have been put to good use. Your keys will have been hidden, the taxi will have been cancelled and leaves will have been placed on the railway track.

Physicists have also fallen foul of a long standing Teddy trick. By inserting a slightly longer beep at the end of the hourly pips on the radio, the Bears have caused clocks all over the world to be wrongly set. The only way of correcting this prank is by having an extra day in the year once every four years - February 29th.

That's not all; have you ever wondered who is responsible for the clocks changing in the summer ? By now it may come as no surprise that furry paws are behind the whole thing. Slick coordination between Bears within each country move clocks back or forwards by an hour on the same day. To cover their tracks, the clever cuddlies also take out small adverts on the front page of most newspapers to tell everybody it is an 'official' change.

TEDDY BEARS

The Secret Lives of

TEDDY BEARS

The Secret Lives of

TEDDY TRUMPS

When a fetid smell wafts into the noses of a group of friends the proclamation is usually "Who did that?", "What have you eaten?" and "You need to take your bottom to a doctor". If the same smell travels round a group who don't know one another so well, there will be a prompt and rapid dispersal of people from the group. Everybody will suspect everybody else of dropping the acrid odour, but nobody will look in the direction of the real culprit - Teddy.

You may think that Teddy lacks sphincter control. Not at all, it is quite the opposite. Bears have an uncanny ability to hold in their body-wind until a suitably embarrassing moment.

Try sitting in an office with just your Teddy for company. Just as your boss walks in to discuss an important point, Teddy will drop one. Alternatively try inviting a new girlfriend or boyfriend round for a meal. You will be on the verge of your first mouthful when a non-edible smell will engulf your nostrils. Never dream of taking your Teddy in your back-pack if you go skiing. Whenever you get in a cable-car, that fateful pong will ooze out of your pack.

Unfortunately for Ted, most bad smells are blamed on the dog. If Ted could think of a way to get the blame for the odours placed on the cat, you could be sure of a lot more wind in your house.

TEDDY BEARS

The Secret Lives of

TEDDY BEARS

The Secret Lives of

BEARS IN SPACE

The first man to walk on the moon was Neil Armstrong on 21st July 1969. But totally unknown to this great and fearless adventurer, he had been beaten to the true glory by his close travelling companion a few hours earlier. While the Space Centre at Houston monitored the famous astronaut's pulse rate during sleep before his historic promenade, his Teddy Bears were already taking a look around outside.

The giant leap for mankind might have been a small step for man, but it was a huge fall for the first Teddy on the stairs. Trying to reach down the final three feet, Neil's Teddy stumbled and fell ears-first onto the surface of the moon. Luckily moon-dust is so soft it broke his fall.

In the white heat of excitement for the human race, the Teddy Bears' paw marks proved too small to be noticed by NASA on subsequent television transmissions. Also unseen, or at least unreported, was the flag the Bears had erected to Snuggleonia just behind the Eagle spacecraft. However, if you study photographs taken of the moon's surface each day, you will notice small craters appear which weren't there the day before. These were created by our mischievous little friends, with their buckets and spades, while the more serious human lunar-explorers slept.

TEDDY BEARS

The Secret Lives of TEDDY BEARS

The Secret Lives of

OIL BEARS

The accepted image of an oil worker is one of a roughy-toughy oil rig tiger battling it out against vicious natural elements to pipe the precious 'black gold' back to our shores. But did you know that most of these roughnecks take their Teddy Bears offshore with them?

After a hard twelve hour shift, an oil-rig's drill crew usually throw a couple of 72 ounce steaks into their stomachs and toddle off to bed for a trip to Snuggleonia with their favourite bed-pals. Once certain that their owners are sound asleep (indicated by a deafening 120 decibel snore) the Bears sneak up to the drill floor. They are then lowered down, in threes, into the bowels of the earth on a piece of drill pipe. With their hard hats on and complete with safety boots, they keep the digging going right through the night before returning to bed to comfort their owners in the morning.

TEDDY TRUTH

A Teddybeer isn't something you stick on the end of a round at the pub, rather it is the Dutch word for Teddy Bear

Next time you switch on a light or plug in a kettle, spare a small thought for all the oil-soaked Teddies flying backwards and forwards in the drafty holds of helicopters.

TEDDY BEARS

The Secret Lives of TEDDY BEARS

The Secret Lives of

PILOT BEARS

Most people have seen a Teddy Bear dressed up in a pilot's uniform, usually in the colours of a particular airline. But not many realise the Bears are responsible for the safe arrival of each carriers' aircraft.

Technically known as 'autopilot', the Bears' role is to keep the plane flying on its desired route while the human pilots have a quick nap. Some specialist Teddy Bears, indicated by a pair of flying goggles which look remarkably like those used by swimming Bears, also have the ability to land an aircraft at night in fog.

TEDDY TRUTH

If somebody asked you to a fancy dress party as a Bear don't turn up with no clothes on, they probably mean you should hire a Teddy Bear costume

On longer flights the air-stewardesses are also required to take a Teddy with them. While they catch up on a bit of sleep and escape the needs of the passengers for a few minutes, their Teddies beaver away in the galley putting the next meal onto lots of little Bear-sized trays. If you ever go on an aeroplane, take a close look at the button which you use to call the stewardess. Sitting proudly on the indicator is a picture of a small Teddy Bear.

TEDDY BEARS

The Secret Lives of TEDDY BEARS

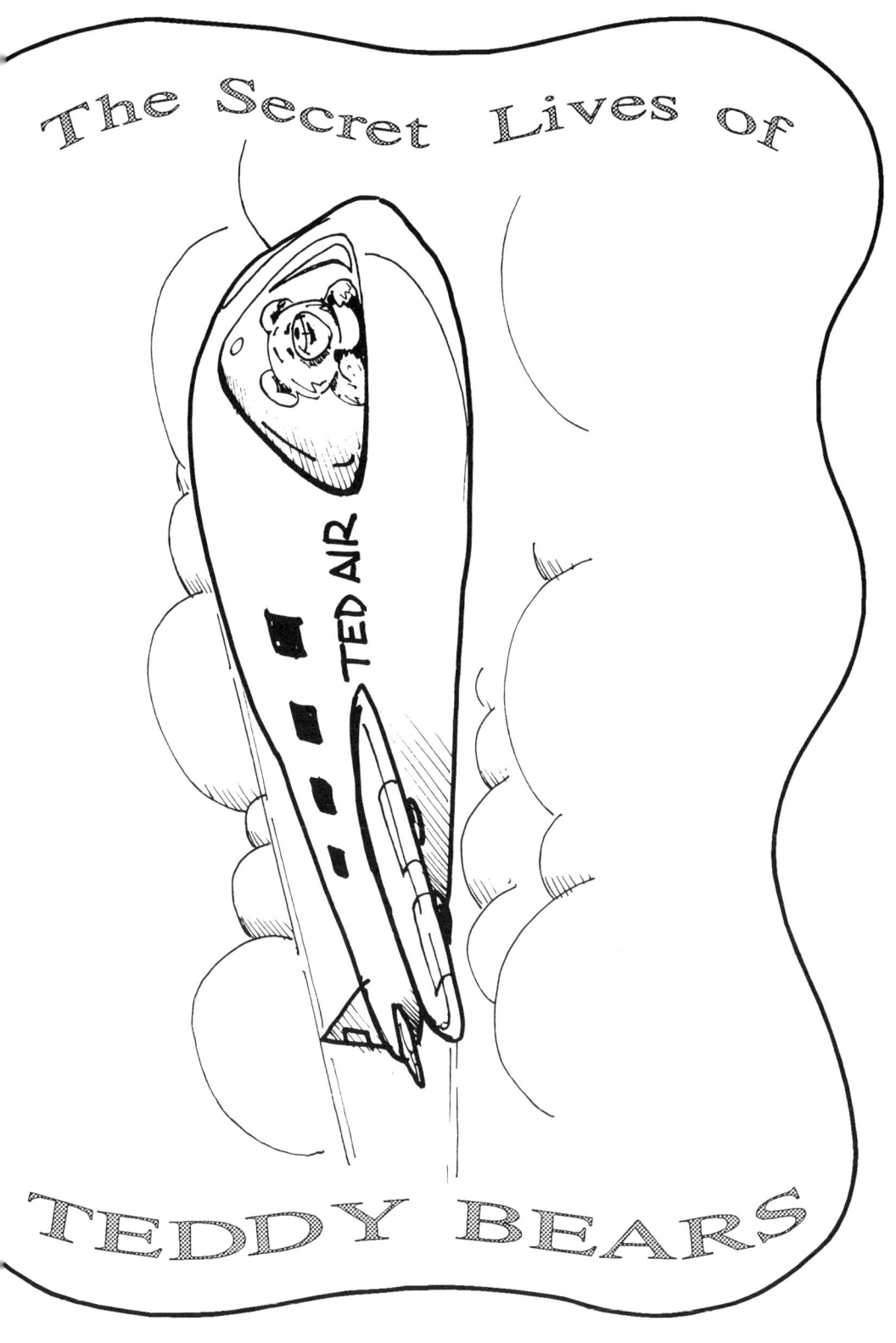

The Secret Lives of

BEARING IT ALL ON FILM

Teddies are all over the big screen and only come second to the hero as the favourite bedmate of the starring actresses. Did you see...

'Sleeping with the Teddy' - Hero Bear has to feign death on a boating holiday to escape the clutches of his evil owner. Owner finds discarded fur in his toilet and gives chase.

'Silence of the Teddies' - Serial Bear thief kidnaps Teddies to make a Bear suit for himself. A convicted Bear eater helps track him down.

'Nightmare in Teddy's Bed' - A killer Bear wearing a cricket box on his face goes around attacking victims while they sleep.

'Terminator Teddy' - Teddy says "I'll be back".

'Star Bears' - Luke Bedwarmer joins forces with the Princess Bear and uses the Bear-force to make war on the evil empire. Luke turns out to be the son of a black Bear called Ted Vader.

'The Elephant Teddy' - Something goes wrong in the Teddy factory face-department.

'Teddy I, II, III & IV' - I Teddy has to fight for his rightful place in the heroines bed; II he is dislodged and has to fight his way back;

TEDDY BEARS

The Secret Lives of Teddy Bears

III Teddy's owner dies and he loses all hope of being happy in bed again, however inspiration from the song 'Eye of the Teddy' gets him another bed; **IV** made during the cold war, Teddy is challenged by a cheap but big Soviet Teddy Bear.

'A Fistful of Teddies' - A quietly spoken and moody Teddy cleans up one of the meanest beds in town, leaving a trail of spaghetti over the sheets.

'The Day of the Teddies' - People are blinded by a meteorite storm which also causes Teddies to grow and take over the world.

'Polter-Teddy' - Teddy walks around at night noisily moving objects and making funny noises.

'Teddy get your Gun' - Hillbilly Ted in dungarees does a bit of dancin' and shootin'.

'Around Snuggleonia in 80 Days' - Ted uses toy trains, party balloons and roller skates to cross the bed and win a bet.

'Top Ted' - Pilot Bear shows off his flying skills to pull his Bearess instructor then contrives a mission against the enemies of Snuggleonia. Cameo role by Ice Bear.

'Wall Street' - Scandal in a Bear market.

'Million Dollar Teddy' - After a particularly bad encounter with the family dog, Teddy is rebuilt with bits of an old children's robot.

'The Teddies from Brazil' - A German Doctor takes his Teddy to Brazil and builds a factory to reproduce it for his pet Doberman.

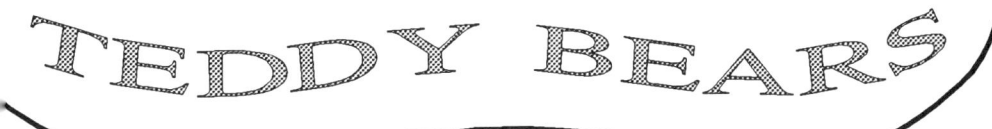

The Secret Lives of TEDDY BEARS

FORMAT HARD DISC

The Secret Lives of

TEDDY BEARS

The Secret Lives of

BEARS ON VINYL

It's not only 'hip' to be seen with a Teddy in a nightclub, but you can also 'hop' to some of their sounds on the dance-floor. The Top Ten Teddy Hits this week are...

1. **Bruce Stitchseam** - Born to pun.

2. **Bear Aid** - Do they know it's bedtime?

3. **Chuck Beary** - Teddy be good.

4. **Deep Pawple** - Bears on the water.

5. **Teddy & The Bears** - Sleeping round the clock.

6. **Baba** - Stuffing me, stuffing you.

7. **Elvis Pawsley** - Bearhouse rock.

8. **The Beartles** - StrawBeary Fields Furever.

9. **Ted Stewart** - Do you think I'm cuddly?

10. **The Seam Pistols** - Never mind the stitching, here's the Teddy Bears.

TEDDY BEARS

The Secret Lives of

PPSSSSSSS!!

TEDDY BEARS

The Secret Lives of

POWER BEAR

Some people say the First Lady is the most powerful person in The White House as a close advisor to the President. However, there is one little confidante who continues to give his opinions long after the First Lady has put in her curlers and slumbered off to the land of nod.

Yes, the President's Teddy is by far the most powerful voice in America. Without the constant support and advice from their Teddies, many past Presidents would have gone completely loopy with all the pressure. **Perhaps you can spot the ex-presidents who didn't have a Teddy as their right hand advisor.**

Apart from the fact that we could all disappear in a flash of nuclear explosions as a result of some Teddy devised prank, it's certainly a lot safer having a Bear in charge. Just think of the state the world would be in if the Presidents had done it their way.

TEDDY TRUTH

The dictionary definition of a Bear is "A heavy partly carnivorous thick-furred plantigrade quadruped." !!
That doesn't sound very cuddly does it ?

TEDDY BEARS

The Secret Lives of

GLUG!
GLUG!
GLUG!

TEDDY BEARS

The Secret Lives of

GAMBLING ALONG

Teddy loves a quick flutter on the horses when he can get into the bookies without being seen. From then on it is easy because the assistants can't see anyone, let alone Teddy Bears, through the haze caused by nervous smokers. So there is no trouble placing a bet even though few Bears can see over the counter.

This love of betting on the 'Sport of Kings' has nothing to do with the wayward practice of gambling under-size. No, it has more to do with the fact that multi-lingual Teddies can talk to horses. There is nothing more sure than a tip from a Teddy Bear which indirectly comes from the horses mouth. So next time your friend says his Teddy Bear has given him a tip for the 2:30, don't call the local loony-bin, get your wallet out instead.

Other sources of income for Bears include betting on football, boxing and general elections. The strong network between Bears allows information to be passed around very quickly. Boxing and football are both fixed by the unfortunate boxer or football team's Teddies keeping them awake the night before the big fight or game. Elections are rigged by Teddies taking a bottle of correction fluid and pen to their owner's speeches.

Where do Bears spend all this income ? They fritter it away on Booze, Bears of the opposite sex, and Bingo.

TEDDY BEARS

The Secret Lives of

TEDDY BEARS

The Secret Lives of

CAT BURGLARS

When a Teddy gets tired of pulling pranks on The Owner, he turns his attention to other households in the street. At first this might consist of ringing door bells and hiding behind the rhododendrons, but later it will escalate into aggravated burglary. Not that anybody gets hurt, they just get aggravated. The objects that go missing aren't even stolen, they are just very well hidden.

Some Bears specialise in this form of 'prank'. When they have finished hiding the valuable objects of a particular street, and when they have parked all the expensive cars in other cities, they will turn their attention to where Owners keep all their money.

A Teddy's size will help it get through most security devices a bank or museum has to offer. They are too light to set off any pressure pads, too short to trigger any laser beams and they don't radiate any infra red. Once inside, the main problem becomes getting enough Bears together to lift the booty and move it to a suitable hiding place.

The consternation and headlines caused by hiding money, gold bars and diamonds in a bank makes all the effort of getting teams of Bears together for the raid seem worthwhile. However, the main delight comes when the prank is blamed on cat-burglars. Anything that's blamed on cats is OK by the Bears.

TEDDY BEARS

The Secret Lives of TEDDY BEARS

The Secret Lives of

BEARS IN SHOPS

Take your Teddy shopping at your peril. In the supermarket a Bear will find a whole host of tricks to play. First and foremost he will tie strings to the shopping trolley. No matter which trolley you get, Teddy will make it behave as if it has a mind of its own by sending it off in random directions.

TEDDY TRUTH
More than 350 songs were copyrighted between 1907 - 1911 with the words "Teddy Bear" in the title.

As you go around the shop, you might think your coat is catching on things. In reality, it is Teddy trying to grab items from the shelf. You will know when he has been successful by the loud crash of a bottle of pickled onions on the ground behind you.

Further round you will find a tin or a packet which seems to be a bargain. By the time you get it to the check-out, Teddy will have replaced the original price label with one showing twice the price.

Also be on your guard when you walk out to the car-park with your purchases. While you are looking for the car which Teddy will have moved, and while you search for the keys he has thrown out of your pocket in the supermarket, you will be stopped by the store detective asking about the items Teddy put in your pocket without paying for them.

TEDDY BEARS

The Secret Lives of

TEDDY BEARS

The Secret Lives of

CHRISTMAS PRESENTS

Christmas day is full of fun for Teddy Bears. It starts off with a good kick in the ribs for all the children to wake them up at around 4 a.m. The presents will already have been changed in the kids' christmas stockings to the noisiest possible, such as drum sets and trumpets.

While you are trying to put the children back to bed, Teddy will sneak down for a quick cuddle with the fairy on top of the tree. On the way back down he will blow the fuses again on the fairy lights. At the bottom he will change the labels on the presents so everybody gets something they have always dreaded. If he has time, he will put the price labels back on the presents and remove any batteries that may have been included.

As the day progresses, Teddy will content himself with jumping in and out of the wrapping paper, making the children seem more interested in the boxes than the presents. He will call up all the relatives you steadfastly try to avoid and invite them over for a long drink. And he will leave a small trail of turkey all the way over to the cat's bed.

Before you go to bed, Teddy will probably have 'phoned the police and complained about the noise coming from your house. He will have spiked all your food with alcohol, so you wake up with a storming headache on boxing day. Plus he will have broken, torn or caused to malfunction as many presents as possible. What a day !

TEDDY BEARS

The Secret Lives of
TEDDY BEARS

The Secret Lives of

CATCH THE LITTLE BLIGHTERS

Private detectives use a simple trick to keep track of suspects. When they want to know whether someone has left a place, they put a coin on the wheel of the fugitive's car. If the coin has gone in the morning, it is possible the person left that location and came back again.

However, if you want to keep track of your Teddy Bear's movements don't use a coin, the Bear will only pinch it. Instead, we recommend that you use the paper disks we have printed below. **Cut out the disks and place them on your Teddy**, then place him on your bed when you go to sleep.

As soon as you wake up, check the paper disks. If they are not exactly where you left them, the Bear has been out of bed creating trouble - so watch out for the rest of the day. You better watch out anyway, because some Teddies are clever enough to remember where the disks were and put them back on.

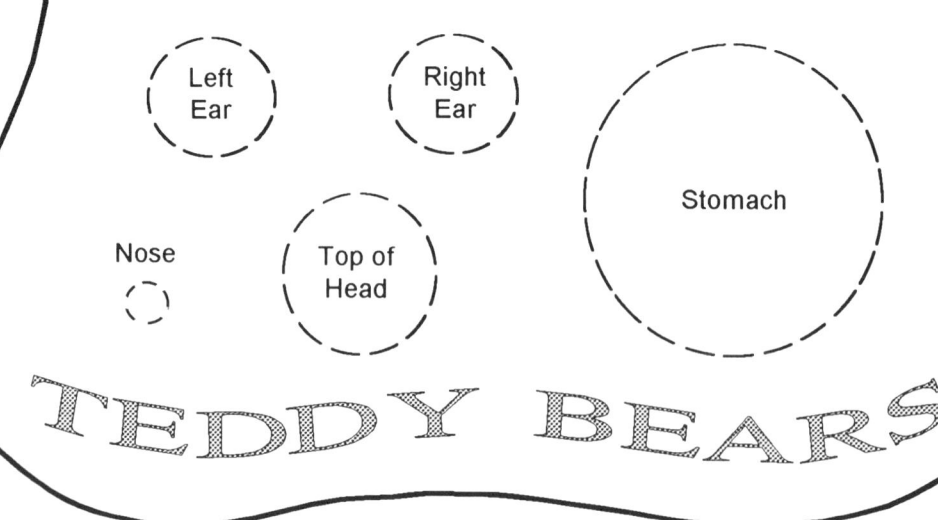

- Left Ear
- Right Ear
- Nose
- Top of Head
- Stomach

TEDDY BEARS

The Secret Lives of

TEDDY BEARS

The Secret Lives of

IDENTITY PARADE

Should anything go wrong in your home or to anything you touch throughout the day, we suggest you give your Teddy Bear a three part interrogation.

First of all, put some ink on your Teddy's paw and press it firmly onto a piece of paper. If it looks anything like the paw prints below, in any size, the Bear is guilty of a misdemeanour of some sort.

Secondly shave your Teddy Bear's hair, like they do to all convicts in the movies. Then put him under a bright lamp and check to see if his eyes are too close together (as per standard police procedures).

Thirdly hold an identity parade. If your Teddy DOES NOT bear any resemblance to the picture of a Teddy below, then he is guilty.

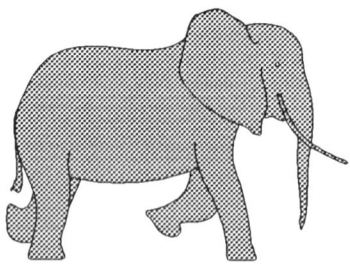

All Bears should be given a fair trial, found guilty and un-stuffed.

TEDDY BEARS

The Secret Lives of TEDDY BEARS

The Secret Lives of 'NATURAL' PHENOMENA

There are many unexplained mysteries of the modern world such as Corn Circles, Unidentified Flying Objects, The Bearmuda Triangle, etc. While many organisations delight in perpetuating myths about alien life forms and extraterrestrial visits, the source of these mysteries is closer to home. In fact, it is probably in your bed.

It has been a constant source of amazement to Teddy Bears as to why scientists flock to their tea parties when they've already finished. Quite simply, the Bears organise a tea-party or picnic in a picturesque field (usually a corn field because the colour of ripe corn camouflages the frolicking Bears during daylight). They have a bit of fun, roll around and then leave. A couple of days later one or two people look at the place where the party took place, take a few photographs and drive off at high speed. Then hundreds of photographers from tabloid newspapers and pseudo-scientists descend on the site.

Unidentified Flying Objects, or UFOs, can be attributed to three of Teddy's pranks. Firstly, Bears are keen makers of paper aeroplanes from pieces of paper they find with important 'phone numbers, addresses or notes on them. Secondly, some of the traps they set for the pet cat are extreme, and cause the said moggy to fly through the air for several metres. Thirdly, Teddy likes to take a look at pictures taken with a camera before they have been developed, sometimes causing strange images to appear on the film when it is developed.

TEDDY BEARS

The Secret Lives of Teddy Bears

A repetitive irony is the fact that many grown adults still take their Teddies along with them if they are afraid. This has proven a costly mistake for many a pilot and sailor in a small triangular region just off the coast of Bearmuda. The more people that are fearful of this triangle, the more vessels that will go missing due to a Teddy Bear escapade.

Modern manufacturing techniques now allow the making of man-sized, or larger, Teddy Bears. So, there should be no surprise when their footprints are found in snow or dirt. Although most Bears go to strenuous efforts to cover their tracks, some large Teddies like to fool Yeti and Bigfoot searchers into visiting inhospitable areas.

Peruvians also have Teddy Bears, and they have had them for many years. Some of these Bears have escaped the clutches of their Owners and now live in the desert near a small town called Nazca. They have developed their own culture and like to make patterns in the sand which can only be seen from the air.

If, at any time in the future, you see or hear of any 'mysterious happenings', check the vicinity for the presence of a small furry being.

The Secret Lives of

TEDDY BEARS

The Secret Lives of

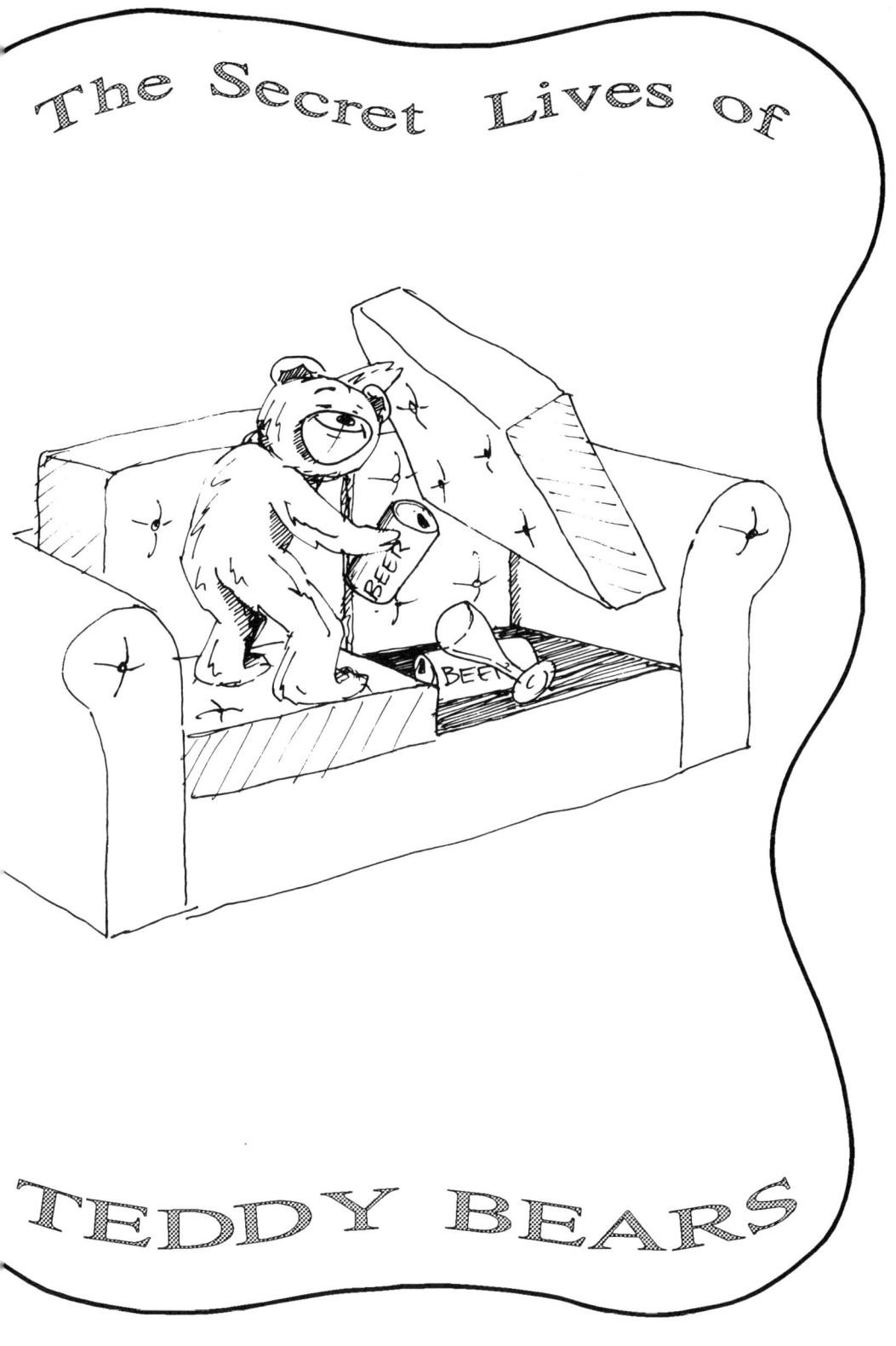

TEDDY BEARS

The Secret Lives of HISTORICAL TEDDIES

THROUGHOUT HISTORY Teddy Bears have helped influence the development of the Human Race. In fact, some would say that we wouldn't have come so far without the valuable assistance of our furry bedtime pals. Is this taking things a bit far ? Well, why not judge for yourself with this A-Z of historical figures who owe at least part of their fame to their Teddy Bears.

A is for Archimedes who, in the 3rd Century BC, dropped his Teddy Bear in the bath and measured the amount of water displaced. The bath was rather big and it took young Archimedes a while to get his Teddy back. When he did, he ran out into the street shouting "Eureka" or "I have it".

B is for Beethoven a second rate musician but for his Teddy. While sitting his music exams, it was Beethoven's habit to place his lucky mascot Teddy on the top of the piano. During one of his harder exams, the little Bear kept falling off and hitting random ivories on the keyboard. The examiners who had been tape-recording Beethoven's efforts while they watched a more promising pupil, judged his work as extremely original and influential, and gave him a recording contract for loads of symphonies.

C is for Julius Caesar whose reign over the Roman Empire came to an unsavoury end when his Teddy 'Brutus' stabbed him in the back.

D is for Salvador Dali who tried to paint the world in the way his Teddies saw it. Not many people understood what he was putting on canvas, but knowing he was a famous painter they commented "That sure is real".

TEDDY BEARS

The Secret Lives of Teddy Bears

E is for Einstein. While trying to patent a flying Teddy, Albert realised that his Teddy was gaining weight and ageing less every time he completed a flight. From this he formulated his theories of relativity which state "Some Teddies are relatively bigger and younger than others".

F is for Henry Ford who was the first person to produce cheap Teddies for the masses. Ford is quoted as saying "You can have any type of Teddy you like, so long as it's furry".

G is for Genghis Khan. After a deprived childhood, Genghis got his first Teddy while he was in his twenties. Incensed by the amount of pleasure he had been missing out on, he decided he would try to make up for lost time and went about stealing every Teddy in the world.

H is for Henry VIII who had five Teddies one after the other because none could satisfy him. Many horrible rumours have been generated about the fate of his Bears, including one which suggests he separated their upper and lower parts. Only his last Bear outlived Henry.

I is for the man in the Iron Mask. This Frenchman was so embarrassed when his friends discovered his Teddies that he spent the rest of his life hiding behind a black silk mask.

J is for Jezebel, a biblical character who betrayed her own Teddy Bears.

K is for Karl Marx who proclaimed that all Teddy Bears should be equal and should also be considered on a level status with humans. Down on his farm, several of Karl's friends agreed with him but thought Bears should be more equal than pigs.

L is for Leonardo de Vinci. After painting a church roof with his Teddy in order to get wide brush strokes, Leonardo promised to paint his girlfriend Mona Lisa. Mona was happy to pose for the picture but was disconcerted that Leonardo used his Teddy to keep her attention. The rather odd smile seen on the finished painting can be attributed to Mona wondering why Leonardo was waiving a Teddy at her which was covered in green paint.

The Secret Lives of

M is for Ferdinand Magellan. The luckless Magellan lost his Teddy and, believing it stolen, set sail to find it again. Only when he had been right round the world did he find it snuggling at the bottom of his toy box.

N is for Napoleon who always kept his hand on his Teddy, even during battle.

O is for Georg Simon Ohm. While doing his physics homework, Ohm accidentally passed electricity through his Teddy Bear. The shock caused all the Bear's hair to fall out. Not surprisingly Teddy resisted any attempts for Ohm to use him in any more of his experiments. This prompted Ohm to formulate his theory of resistance.

P is for Ivan Pavlov. Every time Pavlov went to feed his Teddy Bear, the dog started salivating.

Q is for Quasimodo who kept his Teddy at the top of one of his sleeves. During the day, Quasi would sneak up the local tower and hit his Bear against the bells.

R is for Robin Hood who robbed the rich of their Teddy Bears and distributed them to the poor.

S is for Spartacus. The Romans wanted Spartacus to give up his Teddy Bear when they took him into slavery. Spartacus was aggrieved at this because he didn't think he would be able to sleep at night on his cold stone bed. While the emperors declined his offer to fight them for his Bear, they agreed Spartacus could keep his Teddy if he continued to win gladiatorial contests.

T is for Teddies everywhere.

U is for Uncle Sam, a Teddy who caused a war in the United States in 1812.

V is for Valentino who used his Teddy to bolster his charisma, so he could woo unsuspecting women into his confidence.

TEDDY BEARS

The Secret Lives of

W is for Wellington who finally managed to steal Napoleon's Teddy.

X is for Xerxes the Great who started a war in order to gain the Teddy making capability of Persia. One of his own Teddies became jealous and killed him while he slept.

Y is for Your Teddy - how much has he influenced your life ?

Z is for Zeus, considered the God of Gods by those who envied him his golden Teddy.

TEDDY BEARS

The Secret Lives of TEDDY BEARS

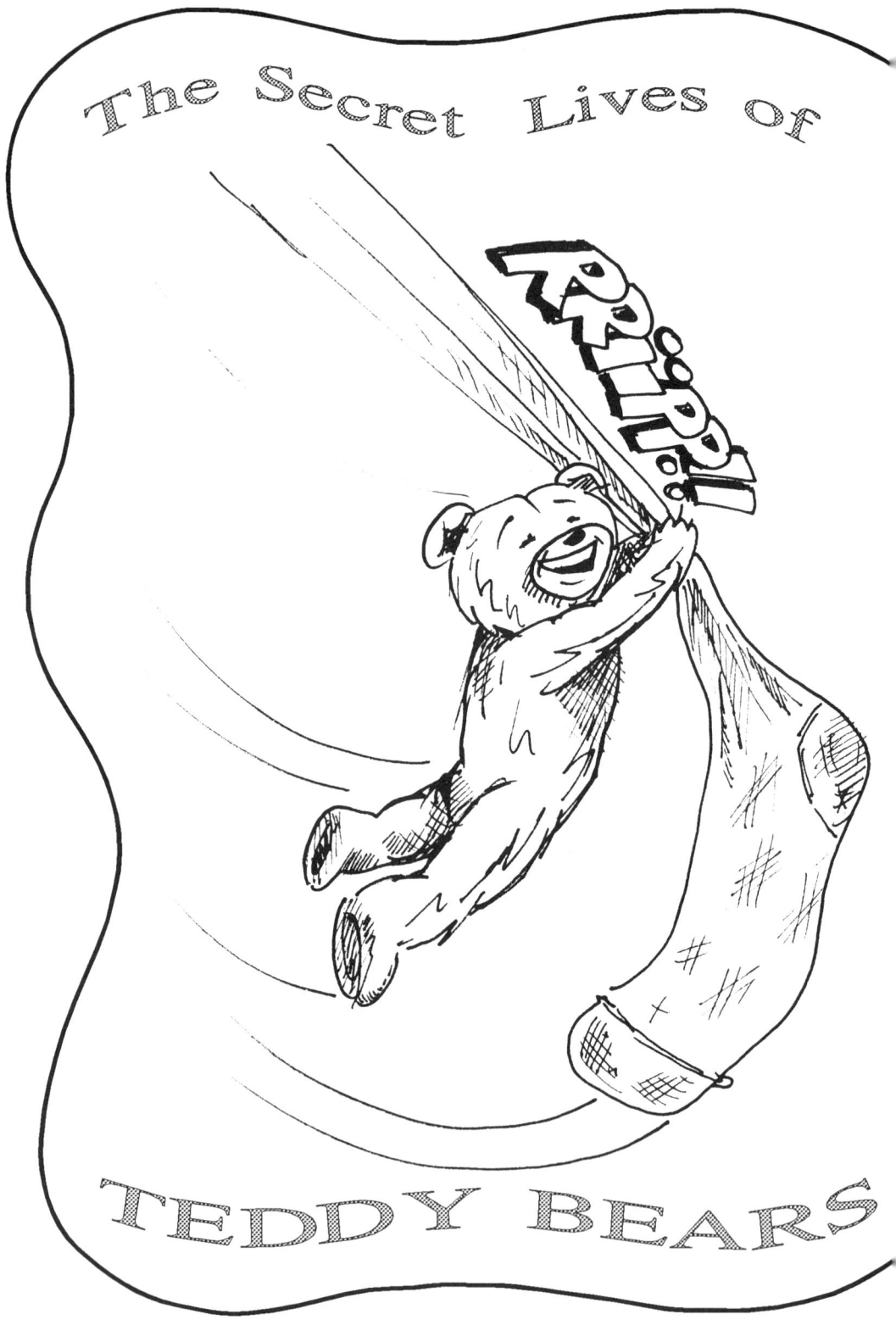

The Secret Lives of

TEDDY BEARS

The Secret Lives of

BEARS IN THE POTTING SHED

Teddy Bears love to mess around in the garden, with the emphasis on mess. No Bear likes the sight of complete order and harmony. They find it offensive to the eye when all the flowers in a bed are colour matched and in perfect little lines. That's why they merrily mix up the seeds in the potting shed before you even plant them. And even if you do get the right seeds in the right beds, Teddy will always manage to plant a strongly growing weed right in the middle of them. Not one single bulb will seem to grow in the place you planted it.

Abandon hope of ever growing an award winning rose or prize marrow. Ted will wander out and lop the heads off anything that looks like being too pretentious. One of his favourite times is early spring. Should the temperatures drop to anything near freezing, Ted will be out snapping off all the new buds and stamping on any shoots poking through the soil. You may also feel like blaming your cat or dog for killing off some of the plants. But before you shout too much at your pet, remember that Teddy likes to relieve himself on your favourite bushes.

And Teddy Bears aren't the only sort of bare you will find in the shed at the bottom of the garden. Many women complain of finding 'girlie' magazines hidden in amongst the gardening manuals and compost. Naturally they blame their husbands and give them a battering with the rolling-pin, without even contemplating that a furry 'friend' may have put them there.

TEDDY BEARS

The Secret Lives of TEDDY BEARS

The Secret Lives of

SPORTSBEARSHIP

Teddies may not have won many major championships or gold medals themselves, but they have certainly been the 'driving' force behind many a great champion.

Of course, their influence on the sporting arena hasn't always been sportsman-like. In fact, many people would call Teddy Bears the ultimate cheats. But, unlike their human counterparts, they do not fix games in order to achieve victory or glory. Their one and only aim is to have a good laugh at someone else's expense.

Some of Teddies favourite sporting pranks are listed below. If any of them have ever happened to you, could your or your opponent's Teddy have tampered with your kit ?

Slackening of Squash or Tennis racquet strings.
Snapping of boot laces just below first hole.
Creating an embarrassing tear in your shorts or singlet.
Filling your running shoes with lead.
Smudging your contact lenses so you can't see.
Throwing away your winning ticket from a side-bet.
Riveting hurdles to the ground.
Loosening tyres on bikes and cars.
Removing wax from skis, and blunting edges.
Photographing ultra-secret keels on racing yachts.
Whispering "out" into cricket umpire's ears.

TEDDY BEARS

The Secret Lives of

Other 'deceptions' are carried out with the 'unsuspecting' help of humans. A prime example is the giving of Teddy Bear shaped covers for golf clubs. You might as well put superglue or chewing gum on each club. No golf ball hit with those clubs will ever fly straight again. The owner will blame the elements, the course or even his own abilities, but he will never know why his skill has apparently deserted him.

If there is someone you have always wanted to beat at a sport, why not give him a Teddy Bear or hide a small Bear in his/her sports bag. At the very least, your opponent will find their shower-gel bottle has leaked all over the bag, and the top will have been knocked off their talc container.

TEDDY BEARS

The Secret Lives of

NURSERY RHYME TEDDIES

Researchers have found that many popular nursery rhymes have actually grown out of more serious situations in history such as plague, pestilence and war. Teddies, as could be expected, have played their part in the formation of these children's rhymes.

Jack and Jill went up the hill, but they didn't suspect that Teddy had drained the well and greased the edges.

Humpty Dumpty sat on the wall until Teddy pushed him off. It was only meant as a joke and he didn't realise the full consequences of his actions. Teddy was forced to lay low for the next three years in hiding from all the Kings men, with only omelette to eat every night.

Hickory Dickory Dock, the mouse ran up the clock around one o'clock. Teddy had got there first and booted it back down.

Baa, baa, black sheep, have you any wool ? Yes sir, yes sir, two bags full (Teddy's stolen one).

A ring, a ring of roses, a pocket full of poses, atishoo !, atishoo !, Teddy's given them all the flu.

TEDDY BEARS

The Secret Lives of

Mary, Mary, quite contrary, how does your garden grow ? With the help of Teddy Bear manure.

Little Jack Horner, sat in a corner, eating his pudding and pie. He stuck in his thumb and pulled out a spanner, and said "Who the heck put that in there ?"

Little Bo Peep lost her sheep because she was stupid enough to leave them with her Teddy Bear.

TEDDY BEARS

The Secret Lives of
LAUGHING BEARS

Teddies are often given to other people as joke presents; after all isn't it funny to see a six-foot wide scaffolder with his Teddy clipped to his belt. However, this form of present giving should not be encouraged - a Teddy is for life, not just for a laugh. More harmless, but still hurtful to the feelings of some of the more sensitive Bears, are the profusion of jokes that have grown up around the furry little beasts. Here are a few so you know which jokes to avoid telling within earshot of your favourite Bears:-

How many Teddies does it take to change a light bulb ? Ten, one to change the light bulb and nine to lift him up to the ceiling.

Why did the Teddy cross the road ? Because the chicken needed comforting.

As the Bishop said to the Actress... you can hold mine if you want to.

What do you call a Teddy with no clothes on ?... Bear.

What is Winnie The Poo's middle name ?... The.

What does DAT stand for ?... Teddies Dyslexia Association.

TEDDY BEARS

The Secret Lives of

How do you start a Teddy Bear race ?... Ready, Teddy, Go !

What do you call a man covered in hair ?... Ted.

How do the police find a mischevious bear ?... They put up One Ted posters.

What do Teddy's wear when they go swimming ?... The bear essentials.

How do you get your money back from a Teddy ?... By reimbearsment.

Who invented relativity ?... Albear Einstein.

What do Bears eat when they are on a diet ?... Yogihurt.

TEDDY BEARS

The Secret Lives of

BEAR QUESTIONNAIRE

What sort of Teddy Bear lover are you? Would you lay down your life to protect your furry bedtime friend, or would you be just as likely to give him to the dog? Do our Bear Questionnaire and find out.

1) You start to share your bed with a new boyfriend/girlfriend, but he/she says they want to share it with you alone and Teddy has to go. Do you:

> A) Throw Teddy away without further thought and get down to some serious nookie.
>
> B) Gently remove Teddy for the evening putting him in a cupboard but putting him back in his rightful place first thing in the morning.
>
> C) Get rid of the jerk, because there are plenty more fish in the sea.

2) You notice Teddy has a bit of jam on his head from your last breakfast in bed. So you:

> A) Find a soft cloth, dampen it a little and gently wipe the jam off.
>
> B) Lick it of and pretend you are giving him a big wet slobbery kiss.
>
> C) Flick different flavour jams all over him and take him along to the local art gallery as a 'modern statement'.

TEDDY BEARS

The Secret Lives of Teddy Bears

3) Your best friend is finding it hard to sleep at night due to emotional problems. Taking your friend quietly to one side you:

> A) Listen to all their problems while keeping hold of your Teddy to prevent you becoming emotionally involved.
>
> B) Smack them over the head as hard as you can with your biggest Teddy, hoping to knock some sense into them.
>
> C) Offer them your favourite Teddy for a few nights while they get over it.

4) You are pulled up in front of your head teacher because you have forgotten to do your maths homework yet again. Do you:

> A) Blame it all on Teddy saying your stupid Bear made you oversleep by altering your clock.
>
> B) Pull out one of your Teddies, perform a song and dance routine with the Bear on the teacher's desk, and hope they notice a brilliant artistic streak to let you off the hook.
>
> C) Let a tear appear in your eye, pull out Teddy, suck your thumb and go for the sympathy vote.

TEDDY TRUTH

The French for Teddy Bear is Nounours

The Secret Lives of

5) When you are in the kitchen cooking, where is your closest Teddy Bear:

    A) Holding open the recipe book while you walk around preparing the ingredients.

    B) Sitting on the side so you can talk to him while you get on with the work and not be thought to be going daft.

    C) In your hand being used to stir the vat of soup because you couldn't find a big enough spoon.

6) A friend decides they need to get a harder street image, which entails throwing away all their Teddy Bears. So you:

    A) Offer every single one of the Teddies a new warm home because you couldn't 'Bear' to see them cast on the rubbish heap.

    B) Ask your friend if you can look through their collection and choose any Teddies that you may want before they are thrown out.

    C) Tell your friend you'll 'get hard' as well, and suggest you have a combined big Bear bonfire.

7) A passing antiques dealer spots your favourite Teddy in your window. He comes to the door and offers to buy the Teddy for a sum which would pay for your next holiday. Do you:

    A) Chase him down the garden path with an umbrella shouting 'Bear abductor' and telling your partner to call the police.

    B) Sound doubtful and gently try to push the deal up to pay for an extra week in the sun.

    C) Pull out a credit card acceptance slip and suggest to the dealer he might like to view the rest of your collection.

TEDDY BEARS

The Secret Lives of

8) Your Mother and Father come to stay for the weekend and say "Don't you think you are a little old for Teddy Bears now ?". You answer by:

> A) Agreeing but pointing out that you only keep them as ornaments and as talking pieces for when friends call.
>
> B) Agreeing and asking them if they know of a local dump or a skip where you could dispose of them.
>
> C) Kicking them both out of your house, saying that the Teddies are better company and more understanding than either of them have ever been.

9) Your house is broken into and your television is stolen. The next day you:

> A) Spend lying in bed afraid to move while clinging to Teddy.
>
> B) Swear revenge, buy an enormous Bear to help guard the house and go out onto the streets in an effort to track down the villains.
>
> C) Curse your bad luck that they took the television instead of your worthless Teddy Bear.

10) The stuffing starts to come out of your Teddy. How do you react:

> A) You rush your Teddy down to the emergency ward of the local hospital and beg the surgeon to put some stitches in immediately.
>
> B) You put a bit of sticky tape over the hole and make a mental note to stich it when you have more time.
>
> C) By pulling the rest of the stuffing out and putting it in a container to save it for the Turkey next Christmas.

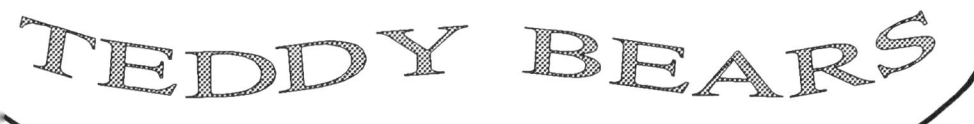

TEDDY BEARS

The Secret Lives of

Make a note of the answers you decided on, look at the points awarded for each answer below and add up your total score.

1) A = 2 points, B = 4 points, C = 6 points.
2) A = 6 points, B = 4 points, C = 2 points.
3) A = 4 points, B = 2 points, C = 6 points.
4) A = 2 points, B = 4 points, C = 6 points.
5) A = 6 points, B = 4 points, C = 2 points.
6) A = 6 points, B = 4 points, C = 2 points.
7) A = 6 points, B = 4 points, C = 2 points.
8) A = 4 points, B = 2 points, C = 6 points.
9) A = 6 points, B = 4 points, C = 2 points.
10) A = 6 points, B = 4 points, C = 2 points.

TEDDY TRUTHS

Rupert The Bear fist appeared in The Daily Express in November 1920
Winnie The Pooh was first published by Methuen in October 1926
Paddington, by Michael Bond, first appeared in 1958

TEDDY TRUTH ?

If you are suffering from Teddyum, it means you are fed up with your Teddy's conversation

TEDDY BEARS

The Secret Lives of

How did you do ?

70 points+   Get back to school and do some more arithmetic practice.

60 points   You are a nutter, but you would be a hero in Snuggleonia. Get certified before it's too late and you could get a cheap bus pass.

41-59 points   Not quite all there are we. A little over obsessive with Teddy Bears. Why not take a trip to the shrink.

21-40 points   A healthy respect for your Teddies and yourself. Stick together and you can take on the world.

20 points   Sicko - what have cuddly little Teddies ever done to harm you ? Let your hair down one day and stop worrying what others think about you.

less than 20   If you didn't want to do the questionnaire in the first place, why are you reading the results ?

TEDDY BEARS

The Secret Lives of TEDDY BEARS

The Secret Lives of Teddy Bears

- **Brain** - for calculating the maximum amount of damage that can be caused.
- **Bobble Nose** - for sniffing out trouble.
- **Ears** - early warning system against humans.
- **Beady Eyes** - for spotting potential pranks.
- **Cute Grin** - for hiding true intentions.
- **Right Paw** - for smearing chocolate on furniture.
- **Stomach** - for poking.
- **Left Paw** - for eating chocolate biscuits.
- **Right Foot** - for kicking cat even harder.
- **Left Foot** - for kicking cat.

Having enjoyed this book, you may like to read one of the following titles which are available by mail-order *post-free*:-

The Ancient Art of Farting by Dr. C.Huff.
Ever since time began, man (not woman) has farted. Does this ability lie behind many of the so far unexplained mysteries of history ? You Bet - because Dr. C.Huff's research shows conclusively there's something rotten about history taught in schools. If you do most of your reading on the throne, then this book is your ideal companion. Sit back and fart yourself silly as you split your sides laughing !

The Hangover Handbook and Boozer's Bible (in the shape of a beercan).
Ever groaned, burped and cursed the morning after, as Vesuvius erupted in your stomach, a bass drummer thumped on your brain and a canary fouled its nest in your throat? Then you need these 100+ hangover remedies. There's an exclusive Hangover Ratings Chart, a Boozer's Calendar, a Hangover Clinic, and you can meet the Great Drunks of History, try the Boozer's Reading Chart, etc., etc.

How to Train Your Cat by Dr. Phee Line (in the shape of a cat).
Educate your moggie to perform simple tricks such as rolling over and begging, through to 'high level' tasks like flying an aeroplane. By careful selection of its natural abilities, you can make your cat perform a useful task around the house (for a change).

How to Get Rid of Your Boss
No matter how much you love your work, there is always one person who makes your professional life a misery - your boss. But all that can change. Find out, with the use of helpful diagrams and cartoons, how to get rid of this person that you despise. It's your chance to get your own back and break free !

The Elvis Spotter's Guide
Strange inconsistencies behind The King's 'death' have lead many fans to believe he is still alive. Now you can track him down with the help of a Priscilla Mask, an instant Elvis Ready Reckoner, 300 amazing Elvis Facts, a 'scoop' of pictures of The King taken since his 'death', cartoons of Elvis in his preferred professions, lists of his favourite meals, cars, girls, etc. And there is a reward of £2 million for the capture of The King. IN COLOUR.

Please return with cheque payment to R&B Publishing, P.O.Box 200, Harrogate, HG29RB
POSTAGE IS FREE within the U.K. Please add £1 per title in other EEC countries and £3 per title elsewhere.

Please send me _____ copies of The Ancient Art of Farting at £3.99 *($A9.95)* each
_____ copies of The Hangover Handbook at £3.99 *($A9.95)* each
_____ copies of How to Train Your Cat at £3.99 *($A9.95)* each
_____ copies of How to Get Rid of Your Boss at £3.99 *($A9.95)*each
_____ copies of The Elvis Spotters Guide at £6.99 *($A14.95)* each

Name:_____ Address:_____

_____ Postcode _____

In Australia, please send payment in $A above (which includes postage) to:
MaxiBooks, P.O.Box 268, Springwood, NSW 2777.